Patricia Acosta
Angela Padrón

# Happy Campers 3

## Student Book

macmillan
education

Macmillan Education
4 Crinan Street
London N1 9XW
A division of Macmillan Publishers Limited

Companies and representatives throughout the world

ISBN 978-0-230-48922-6

Designed by Pronk Media, Inc.
Student Book pages illustrated by: Russ Daff Bee (stories: pp. 20, 36, 44–45, 52–53, 68–69); Scott Burroughs (comic strips: pp. 6–7, 10–11, 18–19, 26–27, 34–35, 42–43, 50–51, 58–59, 66–67); Valentina Mendicino (vocabulary art: pp. 10, 16, 23, 24–25, 26, 32, 34, 39, 40, 42, 48, 50, 55, 56, 58, 64, 66, 71); Pronk Media, Inc. (pp. 8–9, 13, 14, 17, 18, 22, 25, 30, 31, 33, 38–39, 46, 47, 54, 58, 62–63, 65, 70, 72)
Cover design and illustration by Roberto Martínez
Cover photograph by George Contorakes
Picture research by Penelope Bowden, Proudfoot Pictures

The authors and publishers would like to thank the following for permission to reproduce their photographs: **Alamy**/BSIP Sa p. 28(br), Alamy/Go Go Images corporation p. 33(tr), Alamy/David J. Green – Lifestyle p. 9(tr), Alamy/Image Source p. 64(t), Alamy/Juice Images p. 65, Alamy/MBI p. 40(br), Alamy/STOCKCHILDREN p. 40(tl), Alamy/Tetra Images p. 28(tl);
**Bananastock** p. 9(br);
**Corbis**/Monalyn Gracia p. 40(tr);
**Getty Images**/Alistair Berg p. 33(tl), Getty Images/George Doyle p. 64(b), Getty Images/Fuse p. 8(r), Getty Images/Tom Grill p. 28(tr), Getty Images/Jack Hollingsworth p. 12(l), Getty Images/Lucy Lambriex p. 9(bl), Getty Images/Purestock p. 29, Getty Images/Gandee Vasan pp. 12(r), 13;
**Glow Images**/Corbis p. 60(tl), Glow Images/Jamie Grill p. 60(tr);
**Stockbyte** p. 33(br,bl);
**Superstock**/Blend Images p. 40(bl), Superstock/Blue Jean Images p. 17(t), Superstock/Antoine Juliette/Oredia Eurl p. 28(bl), Superstock/Mint Images p. 60(br), Superstock/Stockbroker p. 12(t);
**Thinkstock**/Goodshoot/Jupiterimages p. 60(bl), Thinkstock/iStock/Katarzyna Bialasiewicz p. 61(t), Thinkstock/iStock/Jani Bryson pp. 9(tl), 16, Thinkstock/iStock/julief514 p. 8(l), Thinkstock/iStock/tetmc p. 17(b).

Commissioned photographs by George Contorakes, pp. 5, 14, 22, 24, 30, 38, 46, 48–49, 54, 56–57, 62, 70

The authors and publishers wish to thank the following for their help with the photo shoot: Karen Greer Models, LLC; Anaiya; Angela; Evan; and Sam

Props for commissioned photographs by Luise Johnson-Dailey, Bluwave Creative

Printed and bound in China

2019 2018 2017 2016 2015
10 9 8 7 6 5 4 3 2 1

# Contents

# Scope and Sequence

| Unit | Pages | Vocabulary | Grammar |
|------|-------|-----------|---------|
| 1 | 8–15 | **Numbers:** numbers 10–100<br><br>**Family:** grandparents, parents, aunt, uncle, cousin, niece, nephew | How old is he? He's ninety-nine.<br><br>Who is she? She's my aunt.<br>Who are they?<br>They're my grandparents. |
| 2 | 16–23 | **Months of the Year:** January, February, March, April, May, June, July, August, September, October, November, December<br><br>**Ordinal Numbers:** ordinal numbers 1st–31st | When's your birthday?<br>It's in August.<br><br><br>What's the date today?<br>Today is October fifteenth. |
| 3 | 24–31 | **Times of Day / Adverbs of Time:** in the morning, in the afternoon, in the evening, at night, noon, midnight, early, late<br><br>**Daily Routine:** get up, eat breakfast, go to school, eat lunch, eat dinner, go to bed | What time is it? It's 2 o'clock.<br>It's 2:30. It's noon.<br><br><br>What time do you eat breakfast?<br>At 7 o'clock in the morning. |
| 4 | 32–39 | **Sports:** baseball, basketball, football, golf, ping pong, soccer, tennis, volleyball<br><br>**At Home:** listen to music, talk on the phone, watch TV, take pictures, do homework, work on the computer | I'm (not) playing football.<br>We're (not) playing volleyball.<br><br>He's listening to music.<br>They're doing homework. |
| 5 | 40–47 | **At the Park:** climb trees, have a picnic, play ball, play on the swings, ride a bike, ride a skateboard, run, take a walk<br><br>**Chores:** clean, wash the dishes, sweep the floor, feed the pets, take out the trash, set the table, make a snack, wash the car | What are you doing?<br>I'm (not) riding a bike.<br>We're (not) running.<br><br>What's he doing? He's washing the dishes.<br>What are they doing? They're sweeping. |
| 6 | 48–55 | **Clothes:** T-shirt, pants, cap, shorts, jeans, swimsuit, sandals, sneakers<br><br>**At the Beach:** swim, sleep, fly a kite, sail a boat, eat ice cream, build a sandcastle | What are you wearing? I'm wearing sneakers. Are you wearing shorts?<br>Yes, I am.<br><br>Is she swimming? Yes, she is.<br>She isn't sleeping. |
| 7 | 56–63 | **Party Food:** cake, chips, sandwiches, candy, juice, lemonade, popcorn, soda<br><br>**Party Time:** sing, dance, bake a cake, buy snacks, send invitations, make decorations | Are they eating cake? Yes, they are.<br>Are they drinking soda? No, they aren't.<br><br>We're making decorations.<br>Are you baking a cake?<br>Yes, we are. |
| 8 | 64–71 | **Abilities:** draw, hop, paint, play the guitar, play the drums, jump rope, speak English, whistle<br><br>**Vocabulary Review:** Level 3 verbs | I can play the guitar. I can't whistle.<br><br><br>Can you whistle? Yes, I can. |

| Extra Practice | Teamwork Activity |
|---|---|
| 🏠 **The Language Lodge:** Pages 1–4 <br> 🃏 **Happy Campers app:** Unit 1 | Family Age Line |
| 🏠 **The Language Lodge:** Pages 5–8 <br> 🃏 **Happy Campers app:** Unit 2 | Birthday Calendar |
| 🏠 **The Language Lodge:** Pages 9–12 <br> 🃏 **Happy Campers app:** Unit 3 | Daily Activities Poster |
| 🏠 **The Language Lodge:** Pages 13–16 <br> 🃏 **Happy Campers app:** Unit 4 | Sing and Act |
| 🏠 **The Language Lodge:** Pages 17–20 <br> 🃏 **Happy Campers app:** Unit 5 | Weekly Activities Calendar |
| 🏠 **The Language Lodge:** Pages 21–24 <br> 🃏 **Happy Campers app:** Unit 6 | Favorite Activities Chart |
| 🏠 **The Language Lodge:** Pages 25–28 <br> 🃏 **Happy Campers app:** Unit 7 | Party Jobs Chart |
| 🏠 **The Language Lodge:** Pages 29–32 <br> 🃏 **Happy Campers app:** Unit 8 | Abilities Chart |

The Happy Campers Song
Clap your hands
And move your feet!
Let's have fun,
Dance to the beat!
Happy Campers everywhere!
Happy Campers, hands in the air!
Spin around! Move your feet!
Hands up high! Clap to the beat!

**1** 04 **Listen. Then echo.**

ten **10**

**20** twenty

thirty **30**

**40** forty

fifty **50**

**60** sixty

seventy **70**

**80** eighty

ninety **90**

**100** one hundred

**2** 05 **Listen and check (✓).**

## Young and Old!

How old is she?
Thirty? Forty? Fifty?

How old is he?
Thirty? Forty? Fifty?

1.

☐ She's seventy-two.

☐ She's thirty-five.

**3** Page 1 **The Language Lodge**

# Lesson 2

**1**  05 **Sing:**
**Young and Old!**

**2.**

☐ She's twenty.

☐ She's ten.

☐ He's sixty-seven.

**3.**

☐ He's ninety-nine.

## *Grammar Snapshot!*

How old is she?
She's ten.

How old is he?
He's ninety-nine.

**2** **Read and circle.**

1. How old is he?
   He's thirty.

2. How old is she?
   She's seventy.

3. How old is he?
   He's eighty-eight.

**3** **Point, ask, and answer.**

How old is he?

He's ninety-nine.

**4**  Page 2 **The Language Lodge**

# Lesson 3

# Shutterbugs

**1** Who are the people in the photos?

**2** 06 Read and listen.

**1**

Nice photos, Lisa! Who are they?

They're my parents and my grandparents.

**2**

Who is he? Who is she? She's funny!

He's my uncle. She's my aunt. I'm her favorite niece.

**3** 07 Dictation! Listen and write. Then say.

 1. _____

 2. _____

 3. _____

 4. _____

 5. _____

 6. _____

**4**  Page 3 The Language Lodge

# Lesson 4

**1**  **06** **Listen again to Shutterbugs.**

They're my cousins. He's my mom's favorite nephew.

**3**

Ha! Look at his ears!

And he's my silly friend Tom!

Your *favorite* silly friend!

**4**

**2** *Grammar Snapshot!* **Read and match.**

1. Who is she?          He's my uncle.

2. Who are they?          She's my aunt.

3. Who is he?          They're my parents.

**3**  **08** **Listen and cheer!**

Who is he? He's my uncle!

Who is she? She's my aunt!

Who are they? They're my cousins!

CHEER BOX!

**4**  Page 4   **The Language Lodge**

11

# Lesson 5

**1** **Look and complete.**

Nick has _____ people in his family.

**2**  09 **Read and listen.**

## My Family

Hi, my name is Nick.
I'm nine. This is my family.
Grandpa is sixty, and Grandma is fifty-five.
I love my grandpa. He's funny!
These are my parents.
My mom is a teacher and my dad is a firefighter.
I have a sister. Her name is Sally. She's twelve.

This is my Uncle Eric and my Aunt Eva.
I also have one cousin, Daniel.
Daniel wants to be a chef.
He's twenty-one.

And who is he?
He's Oscar, my cat.
He's five. That's thirty-six
in human years!

# Lesson 6

**1**  **Listen again to My Family.**

**2** **Read and match.**

1. She's twelve.              They're Nick's parents.

2. They're Eric and Eva.      He's Nick's cousin.

3. He's twenty-one.           He's Nick's grandpa.

4. She's a teacher and he's a firefighter.    She's Nick's sister.

5. He's sixty.                They're Nick's aunt and uncle.

**3**  **Say Cheese! Draw a picture of your family.**

**4**  **Writing Time! Write about your picture.**

Hi, my name is _____ . I'm _____ .

This is my family. They're my _____ . _____ is

_____ and _____ is _____ .

# Lesson 7

## Team Up!

**1** **Think about people in your family. Make notes.**

My Family
1. grandpa, Joe, 82
2. sister, Katy, 13

**2** **Share with your team.**

Jim is my brother. He's two.

Katy is my sister. She's thirteen.

**3** **Team up and make a team Family Age Line.**

Joe is my grandpa. He's eighty-two.

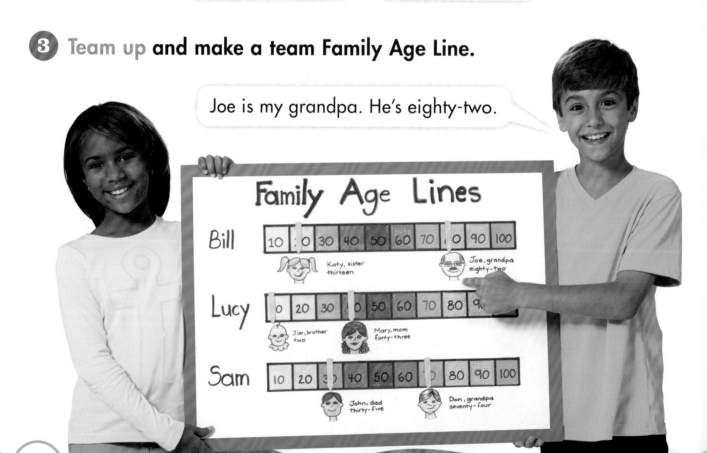

# Lesson 8

**1 Spelling! Write the missing letters.**

1. n e ___ ___ e w

2. ___ n c l ___

3. ___ i e ___ e

4. a ___ n ___

5. ___ o u ___ i ___

6. g ___ ___ n ___ ___ a r ___ ___ t s

**2 Write the words.**

1. **35** _____ - _____

2. **82** _____ - _____

3. **41** _____ - _____

4. **100** _____

**3 Read and match.**

1. How old is she?          She's my aunt.

2. How old is he?          He's thirty-four.

3. Who are they?          He's my cousin.

4. Who is he?          They're my parents.

5. Who is she?          She's fifty-two.

**4 Word Play! Find and circle the words from Unit 1 on Page 72.**

**1**  10 **Listen. Then echo.**

January

February

March

April

May

June

July

August

September

October

November

December

**2**  11 **Listen and complete.**

## Birthday Song!

When's your birthday?
Is it today?
Is it in January, March, or May?

**1.** It's in _____ .

**3**  Page 5 **The Language Lodge**

# Lesson 2

**1**  **11**  **Sing:**
**Birthday Song!**

**2.** It's in _____ .

**3.** It's in _____ .

## Grammar Snapshot!

> When's your birthday?
> It's in August.

**2** **Circle the answer.**

1. When's your birthday?

   **a.** It's in school.

   **b.** It's in July.

2. Use *when* to talk about

   **a.** times.

   **b.** places.

**3** **Ask three friends and complete.**

| Name | Birthday Month |
|------|----------------|
|      |                |
|      |                |
|      |                |

 When's your birthday?

 It's in January.

**4**  **Page 6**  **The Language Lodge**

# Lesson 3

**1** **What month is it?**

**2**  12 **Read and listen.**

**1** Sam, what's the date today? March first?

No, Clare. It's February twenty-ninth.

**2** But February only has twenty-eight days!

There's an extra day this year. Leap Day.

**Shutterbugs**

**3** 13 **Dictation! Listen and match. Then say.**

1. **1st**                fourth

2. **2nd**                first

3. **3rd**                fifth

4. **4th**                second

5. **5th**                third

**4**  Page 7   **The Language Lodge**

18

# Lesson 4

**1**  12 **Listen again to Shutterbugs.**

So today is February thirtieth? March second? Or is it March third?

**3**

No, look at the calendar! It's February twenty-ninth! It's Leap Day!

Sam! I have a great idea for a Leap Day photo!

OK. Say "cheese!"

**4**

Happy Leap Day!

**2** *Grammar Snapshot!* **Complete.**

What's _____ _____ today?

_____ _____ twenty-_____ .

**3**  14 **Listen and cheer!**

What's the date today? Hey, hey!

Today is May eighth. Hey, hey!

CHEER BOX!

**4**  Page 8 **The Language Lodge**

# Lesson 5

**1** **Look and circle.**

This Mayan calendar has

**a.** pictures.          **b.** numbers.

**2**  **Read and listen.**

# The Mayan Calendars

Our calendar has twelve months with twenty-eight, thirty, or thirty-one days. There are many Mayan calendars. One Mayan calendar has nineteen months. Eighteen months have twenty days. But one month has only five days!

The first month in the Mayan calendar is *Pop*.
The nineteenth month is *Wayeb*.

Each month has a picture. The picture for the fourteenth month is a plant under the sun. The sixteenth month has a picture of a different plant.

Some pictures on the Mayan calendar are animals.
The picture for the second month is a frog.
And the sixth month is a dog.

*Kayab* is the seventeenth month.
What animal is it? It's a turtle.
Both calendars have 365 days.
One of those days is your birthday.
When's your birthday?

# Lesson 6

**1** 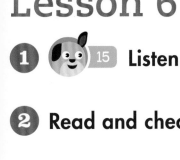 15 **Listen again to The Mayan Calendars.**

**2** **Read and check (✓).**

|  | Mayan calendar | Our calendar | Both calendars |
|---|---|---|---|
| 1. There are nineteen months. | ✓ | | |
| 2. There are 365 days. | | | |
| 3. There is a month called May. | | | |
| 4. There are pictures for each month. | | | |
| 5. There is a frog, a dog, and a turtle. | | | |

**3** **Say Cheese! Draw a picture for the month of your birthday.**

**4**  **Writing Time! Write about your birthday month.**

My birthday is in _____ . _____ is the _____

month of the year. There are _____ days in _____ .

# Lesson 7

# Team Up!

**1** **Think about how your birthday month is special.**

January

April

July

September

**2** **Share your ideas.**

September is in the fall.

April is rainy.

**3** **Team up and make a Birthday Calendar.**

My birthday is
May twenty-second.

## Birthday Calendar

| January | February | March | April |
|---------|----------|-------|-------|
| | | | |
| May | June | July | August |
| | | | |
| September | October | November | December |
| | | | |

# Lesson 8

**1** **Spelling!** **Write the words.**

1. 14th   _fourteenth_

2. 3rd   _____

3. 22nd   _____ - ____

4. 31st   _____ - ____

5. 7th   _____

6. 16th   _____

**2** **Unscramble.**

1.    r a y F b e r u   _____

2.    l r p i A   _____

3.    n u J e   _____

4.    g u t A u s   _____

5.    o v N m e r b e   _____

6.    m e b c e D e r   _____

**3** **Word Play!** **Find and circle the words from Unit 2 on Page 72.**

**1** 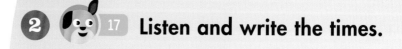 16 **Listen. Then echo.**

in the morning

in the afternoon

in the evening

at night

noon          midnight

early

late

**2** 17 **Listen and write the times.**

## Let's Go!

What time is it? What time is it?
Let's go! Let's go! Let's go!

**3** Page 9 **The Language Lodge**

# Lesson 2

**1**  **17** **Sing: Let's Go!**

1. It's ___12 o'clock___ .

2. It's _____ .

3. It's _____ .

4. It's _____ .

5. It's _____ .

## Grammar Snapshot!

What time is it?
It's noon.
It's 2:30.
It's 2 o'clock in the afternoon.

**2** **Circle the answer.**

1. What time is it?

    **a.** It's 4 o'clock in the morning.

    **b.** In the morning.

2. What time is it?

    **a.** In the evening.

    **b.** It's 3 o'clock in the afternoon.

**3** **Ask and answer.**

 What time is it?

 It's 10 o'clock at night. It's late!

1. 10:00PM    2. 3:00PM

3. 6:00AM    4. 7:00PM

5. 12:00AM    6. 12:00PM

**4** Page 10 **The Language Lodge**

25

# Lesson 3

# Shutterbugs

**1** What is Tom's pet?

**2** 🐶 18 Read and listen.

**1**

*We're late, Tom! What time do you get up?*

BUS STOP

*At 7 o'clock, but I need to eat breakfast before I go to school!*

**2**

*What time do Lisa and Clare eat lunch?*

*At noon. They eat early!*

**3** 🐶 19 **Dictation!** Listen and write. Then say.

 1. _____

 2. _____

 3. _____

 4. _____

 5. _____

 6. _____

**4**   Page 11 **The Language Lodge**

# Lesson 4

**1**   **18 Listen again to Shutterbugs.**

Time to eat dinner!

It's 5:30! What time do you eat dinner?

At 6:00. Bye!

Do your homework, Tom!

This is my Shutterbugs homework.

It's 9 o'clock, Lucy. Time to go to bed!

You too, Tom. Good night!

**2** *Grammar Snapshot!* **Read and match.**

1. What time do they eat lunch?　　At 7 o'clock.

2. What time do you get up?　　At noon.

3. What time do you eat dinner?　　At 6 o'clock.

**3**   **20 Listen and cheer!**

What time do you go to school?

At 7:00! At 7:00! I go to school at 7 o'clock!

**CHEER BOX!**

**4** Page 12 **The Language Lodge**

# Lesson 5

**1** **Circle what the text is about.**

**a.** school          **b.** daily routines

**2** 21 **Read and listen.**

# A School Day

It's 6:00 in the morning. Time to get up!
Children get dressed and eat breakfast.
It's almost time to go to school!

At noon many children eat lunch at school.
They eat in the cafeteria with their friends.
It's a time to relax, eat, and talk.

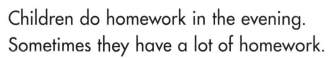

Children do homework in the evening.
Sometimes they have a lot of homework.

At 9 or 10 o'clock at night, many children
go to bed. It's late and it's time to rest.
What a long day!

# Lesson 6

**1** 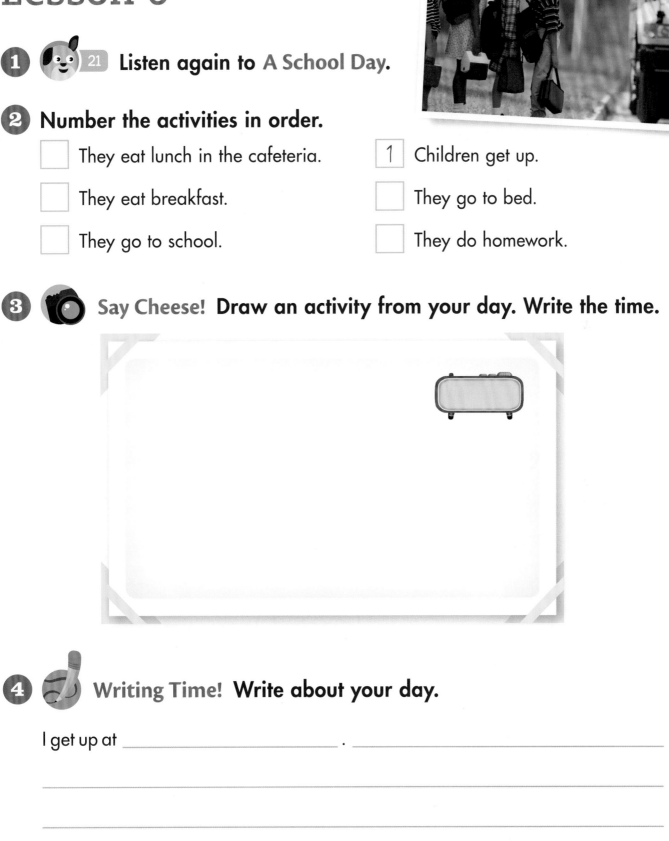 21 **Listen again to** A School Day.

**2** **Number the activities in order.**

| | They eat lunch in the cafeteria. | `1` | Children get up. |

    ☐ They eat lunch in the cafeteria.     ☐1☐ Children get up.

    ☐ They eat breakfast.     ☐ They go to bed.

    ☐ They go to school.     ☐ They do homework.

**3** **Say Cheese! Draw an activity from your day. Write the time.**

**4** **Writing Time! Write about your day.**

I get up at _____ . _____

_____

_____

_____ .

29

# Lesson 7

# Team Up!

**1** **Think about** your day. Make a list of activities and times.

My Day
1. get up: 6:00
2. go to school: 7:00

**2** **Share** your list.

What time do you get up?    At 6:00.

**3** **Team up** and make a Daily Activities Poster.

I go to bed
at 9 o'clock.

# Lesson 8

**1** Spelling! **Write the times of day.**

1. It's 5:00 in the morning                    .

2. _____ .

3. _____ .

4. _____ .

**2** **Read and match.**

1. What time do you get up?            Late. At 10:00 at night.

2. What time do you go to school?      At noon.

3. What time do you go to bed?         Early. At 6:00 in the morning.

4. What time do you do homework?       At 8:00 in the morning.

5. What time do you eat lunch?         At 7:00 in the evening.

**3** **Word Play!** **Find and circle the words from Unit 3 on Page 72.**

**1**  22 **Listen. Then echo.**

baseball

basketball

football

golf

ping pong

soccer

tennis

volleyball

**2**  23 **Listen and complete.**

## Let's Play!

**1.** I'm not playing _____ .

I'm playing _____ .

_____ is fun!

Let's play!

**2.** We're not playing _____ .

We're playing _____ .

_____ is fun!

Let's play!

**3.** We're not playing _____ .

We're playing _____ .

_____ is fun!

Let's play!

**3**  Page 13   **The Language Lodge**

# Lesson 2

**1** 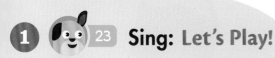 Sing: **Let's Play!**

## Grammar Snapshot!

I'm playing basketball.
I'm not playing football.
We're playing baseball.
We're not playing volleyball.

**2** **Look. Then read and circle.**

1. **a.** I'm playing tennis.
   **b.** We're playing tennis.

2. **a.** I'm not playing golf.
   **b.** We're not playing golf.

**3** **Complete.**

1. We / baseball ❌

   <u>We're not playing baseball</u> .

2. I / golf ✅

   _____.

3. I / soccer ❌

   _____.

**4**  Page 14 **The Language Lodge**

33

# Lesson 3

## Shutterbugs

**1** What is Lisa's grandma doing?

**2**  24 Read and listen.

**1** Hi, Mom, I need to take a family picture. Where is Dad?

He's reading and listening to music.

**2** Hi, Dad. I need a family picture. Where are Jack and Holly?

Jack is doing his homework and Holly is talking on the phone.

**3**  25 Dictation! Listen and write. Then say.

 1. _____

 2. _____

 3. _____

 4. _____

 5. _____

6. _____

**4**   Page 15 The Language Lodge

# Lesson 4

Jack, I need a family picture. Where is Grandma?

Look at Suki! She's watching TV!

She's working on the computer!

OK! I'm taking the picture now. Say "cheese!"

**2** *Grammar Snapshot!* **Complete.**

1. Jack _____ his homework.

2. Grandma _____ on the computer.

3. Suki _____ TV.

**3**  26 **Listen and cheer!**

He's reading a book. She's watching TV.
She's talking on the phone.
At home, home, home!

CHEER BOX!

**4**  Page 16 **The Language Lodge**

35

# Lesson 5

**1** Circle what they're playing in the park.

**a.** baseball          **b.** soccer

**2** 🐶 27 Read and listen.

# Fun in the Park

Sara is at the park.
Her friend Bella is at home.
"Come to the park, Bella!"

"Paul, Will, and Annie are here.
We're playing soccer and listening to music.
We need you! Please come!"

"Thanks, Sara, but I can't play soccer today.
I'm watching TV."

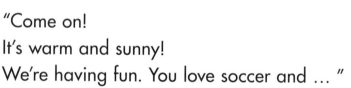

"Come on!
It's warm and sunny!
We're having fun. You love soccer and ... "

"But, Sara, my leg!"
"Oh! That's right. Get well soon!"

# Lesson 6

**1**  **Listen again to** Fun in the Park.

**2** **Circle** *True* **or** *False.*

    **1.** Sara is listening to music.                  True      False

    **2.** Paul, Will, and Annie are playing basketball.     True      False

    **3.** Bella is playing soccer.                     True      False

**3**  **Say Cheese!** **Draw you and your friends at the park.**

**4** **Writing Time!** **Write about your picture.**

Come to the park! I'm _____ and _____ is playing

_____ . _____ is _____

_____ . We're not _____ today.

# Lesson 7

## Team Up!

**1** **Think about** activities you like. **Write a new verse for the song.**

Let's Play!
We're not playing soccer.
We're playing baseball.

**2** **Share** your verse.

> We're not playing soccer.

**3** **Team up** and sing your team song. Act it out.

> We're playing baseball.

# Lesson 8

## Round Up!

**1** **Spelling!** Write the missing double letters.

1.

so_____er

2.

te____ ____i s

3.

b a s k e t b a____ ____

4.

vo_____ e y b a_____

**2** **Read and match.**

1. I'm playing football.

2. We're playing soccer.

3. He's listening to music.

4. She's doing homework.

**3** **Word Play!** Find and circle the words from Unit 4 on Page 72.

**1** 28 **Listen. Then echo.**

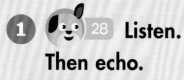
climb trees

have a picnic

play ball

play on the swings

ride a bike

ride a skateboard

run

take a walk

**2** 29 **Listen and check (✓) or cross (✗). Then circle.**

taking a walk

playing on the swings

running

riding bikes

**3** Page 17 **The Language Lodge**

# Lesson 2

**1**  **Sing:** In the Park.

## In the Park

1. What are you doing
   In the park today?
   I'm / I'm not  taking a walk
   In the park today.
   I'm / I'm not  playing on the swings
   In the park today.

2. What are you doing
   In the park today?
   We're / We're not  running
   In the park today.
   We're / We're not  riding bikes
   In the park today.

## Grammar Snapshot!

What are you doing?
I'm playing on the swings.
I'm not taking a walk.
We're riding bikes.
We're not running.

**2** **Circle the answer.**

1. What are you doing?
   **a.** I'm running.
   **b.** He's playing on the swings.

2. What are you doing?
   **a.** They're playing ball.
   **b.** We're climbing trees.

3. We can answer the question
   *What are you doing?* with
   **a.** *I* and *We.*
   **b.** *He* and *They.*

**3** **Complete.**

1. What _____?
   I _____ picnic.

2. What _____?
   We _____ skateboards.

**4**   Page 18  **The Language Lodge**

# Lesson 3

**Shutterbugs**

**1** Is Tom helping?

**2**  30 Read and listen.

1

What are they doing?

They're washing the car. But Tom is washing his hair, too!

2

What's Tom doing now?

He's taking out the trash.

And I'm cleaning up!

**3**  31 **Dictation!** Listen and write. Then say.

 1. _____

 2. _____

 3. _____

 4. _____

 5. _____

 6. _____

 7. _____

 8. _____

**4**  Page 19 **The Language Lodge**

# Lesson 4

**1**  **30** **Listen again to Shutterbugs.**

Tom is washing the dishes. What's Clare doing?

**3**

She's setting the table. We're making a snack.

Oh, no!

**4**

Now what's Tom doing?

He's sweeping the floor.

**5**

No! I'm feeding the pets!

**2** *Grammar Snapshot!* **Match.**

1. What are they doing?          She's setting the table.

2. What's he doing?              They're washing the car.

3. What's she doing?             He's washing the dishes.

**3**  **32** **Listen and cheer!**

What's he doing? He's washing the dishes!

What are they doing? They're making a snack!

CHEER BOX!

**4**  **Page 20** **The Language Lodge**

43

# Lesson 5

**1** **Look and circle *True* or *False*.**

The children like to do chores.  True  False

**2**  **Read and listen.**

# Chores Are Fun!

Kendra and Seth are riding bikes. Zack is taking out the trash. "Dad is making a snack. Let's do chores and then eat!" Zack says.

"I'm not doing chores. Chores aren't fun!" Seth says.

Kendra and Seth are playing ball. Zack is washing the car. Kendra wants to help Zack. She wants a snack, too. But Seth doesn't like chores.

Kendra is cleaning and Zack is sweeping the floor. Seth smells the cookies. Now he wants to help. He's setting the table.

Zack, Kendra, and Seth are eating the snacks and taking a walk. "See, Seth, chores are fun!" Zack says.

# Lesson 6

**1**  33 **Listen again to** Chores Are Fun!

**2** **Number the events in order.**

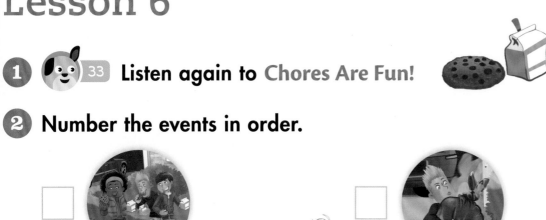

**3** **Say Cheese!** **Draw you and your friends doing chores.**

**4** **Writing Time!** **Write about your picture.**

Today we're _____

_____

_____ .

# Lesson 7

# Team Up!

**1** **Think about your week. Write about four activities.**

| Day | Activity |
|---|---|
| Monday | set the table |
| | |
| | |
| | |

**2** **Share your chart.**

> It's Monday. What are you doing?

> I'm setting the table.

**3** **Team up and make a Weekly Activities Calendar.**

> It's Wednesday. Nick's feeding the pets.

# Lesson 8

# Round Up!

**1** **Spelling!** **Write the *-ing* form of the verbs.**

1. take _____ taking _____

2. make _____

3. set _____

4. run _____

5. sweep _____

6. feed _____

**2** **Check (✓) the correct place for the activity.**

|  | At Home | At the Park |
|---|---|---|
| They're taking a walk. |  | ✓ |
| He's setting the table. |  |  |
| She's sweeping the floor. |  |  |
| They're playing on the swings. |  |  |
| They're having a picnic. |  |  |
| She's washing the car. |  |  |

**3** **Look and answer.**

1. What's she doing?

_____ .

2. What are they doing?

_____ .

**4** **Word Play!** **Find and circle the words from Unit 5 on Page 72.**

**1**  34 **Listen. Then echo.**

**2** 35 **Listen and complete. Then number.**

T-shirt

pants

cap

shorts

jeans

swimsuit

sandals

sneakers

**3**  Page 21 **The Language Lodge**

# Lesson 2

**1**  **35** **Sing:** My Clothes.

## My Clothes

1. What are you wearing?
   I'm wearing a _____ .
   Are you wearing shorts?
   Yes, I am.

2. What are you wearing?
   I'm wearing _____ .
   Are you wearing a cap?
   No, I'm not.

3. What are you wearing?
   I'm wearing a _____ .
   Are you wearing jeans?
   No, I'm not.

## *Grammar Snapshot!*

What are you wearing?
I'm wearing sneakers.

Are you wearing shorts?
Yes, I am. / No, I'm not.

**2** **Circle the question with a *yes/no* answer.**

a. What are you wearing?

b. Are you wearing shoes?

**3** **Circle the answer.**

1. What are you wearing?

   a. I'm wearing a cap.

   b. Yes, I am.

2. Are you wearing sandals?

   a. No, I'm not.

   b. I'm wearing a T-shirt.

3. What are you wearing?

   a. No, I'm not.

   b. I'm wearing sneakers.

**4**  Page 22 **The Language Lodge**

49

# Lesson 3

**1** Where are the Shutterbugs?

**2**  36 Read and listen.

> Where's Tom? Is he flying a kite?

> No, he isn't.

> Is Tom swimming? Is he sailing a boat?

> No, and he isn't eating ice cream. Too bad! Yum!

**3**  37 Dictation! Listen and write. Then say.

 1. _____

 2. _____

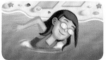 3. _____

 4. _____

 5. _____

 6. _____

_____

**4**  Page 23 The Language Lodge

# Lesson 4

**1**   **Listen again to Shutterbugs.**

Look! Sam is building a sandcastle!

3

Hey! My ice cream!

Is Tom sleeping?

4

Yes, he is! And look! There's my ice cream!

**2** *Grammar Snapshot!* **Write the answers.**

 **1.** Is he building a sandcastle?

Yes, he is                .

 **2.** Is she eating ice cream?

_____ .

 **3.** Is she swimming?

_____ .

 **4.** Is he sleeping?

_____ .

**3**  **Listen and cheer!**

Is he sailing a boat? Yes, he is! Yes, he is!

Is she eating ice cream? No, she isn't! No, she isn't!

**4**   Page 24 **The Language Lodge**

# Lesson 5

**1** Circle where the family is.

   **a.** at the park          **b.** at the lake

**2**  **Read and listen.**

# Fun with Grandpa

It's hot and sunny. Eddie, Lily, Mom, and Grandpa are at the lake.
What's Grandpa wearing?
Is he wearing a jacket and pants?
Yes, he is! Oh, Grandpa!

Is Eddie building a sandcastle?
Yes, he is!
Lily isn't building a sandcastle.
She's flying a kite with Mom.

Eddie wants to swim with his sister, Lily.
"Let's swim, Lily! Come on, Grandpa!"

Look! Grandpa is swimming in his clothes!
He's wearing pants and a jacket.
He isn't wearing a swimsuit.
Eddie and Lily are having fun with Grandpa!

# Lesson 6

**1** 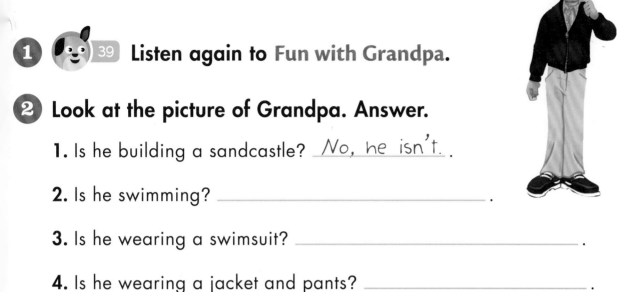 **39** **Listen again to Fun with Grandpa.**

**2** **Look at the picture of Grandpa. Answer.**

**1.** Is he building a sandcastle? _No, he isn't_ .

**2.** Is he swimming? _____ .

**3.** Is he wearing a swimsuit? _____ .

**4.** Is he wearing a jacket and pants? _____ .

**3**  **Say Cheese!** **Draw your family at the lake.**

**4**  **Writing Time!** **Write about your picture.**

It's hot and sunny. _____ , _____ , _____ ,

and I are at the lake. What's _____ wearing? Is _____

wearing _____ and _____ ? _____ .

53

# Lesson 7

## Team Up!

**1** **Think about** your favorite activities.
Number them from 1 to 10. 1 = your favorite activity.

> My Favorite Activities
> 1. eat ice cream
> 2. fly a kite
> 3. clean

**2** **Share** your ideas.

> Eating ice cream is my favorite activity.

> My favorite activity is flying a kite.

**3** **Team up** and make a Favorite Activities Chart.

> Eating ice cream is our favorite activity.

Favorite Activities

eating ice cream    cleaning    flying a kite    riding a skateboard

# Lesson 8

**1** Spelling! **Write the *-ing* form of the verbs.**

**1.** eat _____  **2.** fly _____

**3.** swim _____  **4.** ride _____

**5.** build _____  **6.** watch _____

**2** **Complete the puzzle.**

1.

2.

3.

4.

5.

6.

**3** Word Play! **Find and circle the words from Unit 6 on Page 72.**

**1**  40 **Listen. Then echo.**

cake

chips

sandwiches

candy

juice

lemonade

popcorn

soda

**2** 41 **Listen and complete.**

## There's a Party!

There's a party going on!
Hey! Hey!

There's a party going on!
Hey! Hey!

**1.** Are they eating _____?
Yes, they are.
They're eating _____!

**3**  **Page 25** **The Language Lodge**

# Lesson 2

**1**  41 **Sing:**
**There's a Party!**

**2.** Are they drinking _____?
No, they aren't.
They aren't drinking _____!

**3.** Are they eating _____?
Yes, they are.
They're eating _____!

## Grammar Snapshot!

> Are they eating cake?
> Yes, they are.
> No, they aren't.

**2** **Circle the answer.**

1. Are they drinking soda?
   **a.** No, they aren't.
   **b.** They aren't drinking juice.

2. What are they eating?
   **a.** Yes, they are.
   **b.** They're eating cake.

**3** **Write questions.**

1. They're eating popcorn.
   _Are they eating popcorn_ ?

2. They're washing the dishes.
   _____
   _____ ?

3. They're drinking lemonade.
   _____
   _____ ?

4. They're taking a walk.
   _____
   _____ ?

**4**  Page 26 **The Language Lodge**

# Lesson 3

**Shutterbugs**

**1** Are they preparing for a celebration?

**2** 🐶 42 Read and listen.

Are you sending the invitations?

Yes, we are! Look! Tom is making decorations.

**3** 🐶 43 **Dictation!** Listen and write. Then say.

 1. _____

 2. _____

 3. _____

 4. _____

 5. _____

 6. _____

**4**   Page 27 **The Language Lodge**

# Lesson 4

**1**  **42 Listen again to Shutterbugs.**

We need lots of food. Let's buy snacks and a cake!

**3**

No! Let's bake a cake!

Are you OK, girls? Are you running?

Oh! Fun!

No, we aren't! We're singing and dancing!

**4**

**2** *Grammar Snapshot!* **Circle.**

1. We're sending invitations.

Yes, we are.

No, we aren't.

2. Are you running?

Yes, we are.

No, we aren't.

**3**  **44 Listen and cheer!**

Are you buying snacks? Yes, we are!
Are you baking a cake? No, we aren't.
We're dancing and singing. It's party time!

CHEER BOX!

**4**  **Page 28** **The Language Lodge**

# Lesson 5

**1** **Look and circle *True* or *False*.**

The children are sad.     True     False

**2** 45 **Read and listen.**

## Party Time!

All children love parties!
What's she doing?
She's making decorations.
Look at all the fun colors.

They're playing party games.
They're happy.
What are your favorite party games?

The children are eating a lot of party food.
They're eating salad, and fruit, too.
It looks delicious!

Now they're dancing and singing.
They're listening to music and having fun!
It's party time!

# Lesson 6

**1**  **Listen again to Party Time!**

**2** **Circle *True* or *False*.**

1. She's making decorations.        True        False

2. They're sending invitations.        True        False

3. They're eating breakfast.        True        False

4. They're dancing and singing.        True        False

**3**  **Say Cheese!** **Draw your friends at a party.**

**4**  **Writing Time!** **Write about your picture.**

What are they doing? They're _____ .

They're eating a lot of _____ and _____ .

They're _____ . It's party time!

# Lesson 7

# Team Up!

**1** **Think about** party preparations. Make a list of things to do.

Party Preparations
bake a cake
make decorations

**2** **Share** your list. Act out the party preparations.

Are you baking a cake?

Yes, I am.

**3** **Team up** and make a Party Jobs Chart.

I'm washing the dishes.

| PARTY JOBS | |
| --- | --- |
| Job | Who |
| 🎂 bake a cake | Charlie |
| 🎈 make decorations | Sarah |
| ✉️ send invitations | Tom |
| 🍿 buy snacks | Katy |
| 🧽 wash the dishes | Jack |

# Lesson 8

## Round Up!

**1** **Spelling!** **Complete the words.**

| 1 = a | 2 = b | 3 = c | 4 = d | 5 = e | 6 = f | 7 = g |
|-------|-------|-------|-------|-------|-------|-------|
| 8 = h | 9 = i | 10 = j | 11 = k | 12 = l | 13 = m | 14 = n |
| 15 = o | 16 = p | 17 = q | 18 = r | 19 = s | 20 = t | 21 = u |
| 22 = v | 23 = w | 24 = x | 25 = y | 26 = z | | |

1. ___ ___ ___ ___ ___
   12    13    14   1      5

2. ___ ___ ___
   3     9   16

3. ___ ___ ___
   10   21       5

4. ___ ___ ___
   19           11   19

5. ___ ___ ___ ___ ___ ___
   4     3   15   18              14

**2** **Complete.**

1. _Are_ you _baking_ a cake?    Yes, we _are_ .

2. _____ they _____ decorations?    No, they _____ .

3. _____ invitations?    _____ , we aren't.

4. _____ snacks?    _____ , they are.

**3** **Word Play!** **Find and circle the words from Unit 7 on Page 72.**

**1**  46 **Listen. Then echo.**

draw

hop

paint

play the guitar

play the drums

jump rope

speak English

whistle

**2** 47 **Listen and complete. Then number.**

☐ play the guitar

☐ play the drums

**3**  Page 29 **The Language Lodge**

# Lesson 2

**1**   **47** **Sing:**
All Day Long!

I can play the guitar.

I can't whistle.

## All Day Long! ♪

I can _____
All day long!
I can _____
And sing this song.
But I can't whistle
All day long.
I can't whistle and sing
this song.

**2** **Match.**

**1.** I can draw.

**2.** I can't draw.

jump rope

**3** **Talk to a friend.**

I can't play the drums.

I can speak English.

**4**  **Page 30** **The Language Lodge**

# Lesson 3

Shutterbugs

**1** Can Lisa ride a skateboard?

**2** 🐶 48 **Read and listen.**

**1** Let's take some pictures. Lisa, can you climb trees?

Yes, I can! Look!

**2** Can you play the guitar?

Yes, I can! Listen!

**3** 🐶 49 **Dictation! Listen and write. Then say.**

 1. _____

 2. _____

 3. _____

 4. _____

 5. _____

 6. _____

**4**  Page 31 **The Language Lodge**

# Lesson 4

**1**  48 **Listen again to Shutterbugs.**

**2** *Grammar Snapshot!* **Answer for Lisa.**

**1.** Can you play the guitar? _____ .

**2.** Can you jump rope? _____ .

**3.** Can you ride a skateboard? _____ .

**3** 50 **Listen and cheer!**

Yeah, yeah! Can you draw? Yes, I can. I can draw.

Hey, hey! Can you paint? No, I can't. I can't paint.

**4** Page 32 **The Language Lodge**

# Lesson 5

**1** **Circle what the family is making.**

**a.** a tree house      **b.** a table

**2** 51 **Read and listen.**

# I Can Help, Too!

It's Saturday. Daniel, Tina, and their dog
Bruno are very happy. Mom and Dad
are building a tree house.
"I can help, Mom!" Tina says.
"I can help, too, Dad!" Daniel says.

Daniel can help. There are so many
things that he can do!
Daniel can climb trees. He can help
paint the tree house.
Daniel can also ride a bike. He can
go to the store.

Tina wants to help, too. She can't climb trees.
She can't ride a bike to the store.
But she can draw. She can make decorations.
She can make sandwiches for the family.

What can Bruno do?
Look! He can help, too!
He can eat the sandwiches!

# Lesson 6

**1**  **Listen again to I Can Help, Too!**

**2** **Read and circle Tina's answers.**

| | | |
|---|---|---|
| **1.** Can you climb trees? | Yes, I can. | No, I can't. |
| **2.** Can you draw pictures? | Yes, I can. | No, I can't. |
| **3.** Can you make sandwiches? | Yes, I can. | No, I can't. |
| **4.** Can you ride a bike? | Yes, I can. | No, I can't. |

**3**  **Say Cheese!** **Draw your family building a tree house.**

**4**  **Writing Time!** **Write about your picture.**

It's Saturday. _____ , _____ , _____ ,

and I are very happy. _____ and _____ are building

a tree house. I can _____ . I can't _____ .

# Lesson 7

## Team Up!

**1** Think about **four activities you can and can't do. Make a list.**

| I can | I can't |
|-------|---------|

**2** Share **your ideas.**

Can you play the drums?

No, I can't.

**3** Team up **and make an Abilities Chart.**

We can all whistle.

Leo and Ann can't play tennis.

### CAN ✔

| Activity | Who |
|----------|-----|
| whistle | we can |
| draw | Lucy Ann |
| climb trees | Charlie Leo |
| play tennis | Lucy Charlie |

### CAN'T ✗

| Activity | Who |
|----------|-----|
| play drums | we can't |
| draw | Charlie Leo |
| climb trees | Ann Lucy |
| play tennis | Leo Ann |

# Lesson 8

**1** **Spelling!** **Unscramble.**

1. h i l t w s e  _____

2. i p t n a  _____

3. s k a p e  E i h g n l s  _____  _____

4. y p a l  h e t  r m d s u  _____  _____  _____

**2** **Find and circle the activities.**

| S | A | K | H | O | P | A | E | I | M | W | O |
|---|---|---|---|---|---|---|---|---|---|---|---|
| W | P | B | V | Y | U | F | B | A | T | H | W |
| I | Y | A | R | I | C | S | I | N | G | I | H |
| M | D | T | A | T | A | E | Y | Q | M | S | S |
| R | I | D | E | A | B | I | K | E | D | T | Z |
| A | V | U | F | H | Z | X | G | N | B | L | D |
| Z | L | L | P | A | I | N | T | G | C | E | A |
| W | B | V | A | I | J | P | I | M | H | U | N |
| Q | Y | X | I | H | B | R | G | W | I | R | C |
| P | L | A | Y | G | U | I | T | A | R | X | E |

**3** **Word Play!** **Find and circle the words from Unit 8 on Page 72.**

# Word Play!

soccer
sandwiches
dance
play on the swings
sixth
volleyball
October
sneakers
thirty
bake a cake
twenty
wash the car
sweep the floor
fifth
August

climb trees
June fourth
hop second nephew
eat lunch
whistle
take out the trash
sing
send invitations
late
soda
February
January
make decorations
sandals
April
March
Popcorn
work on the computer
ten
swimsuit
eat ice cream
midnight
noon
seventy
candy
baseball
feed the pets
have a picnic
chips
forty
uncle
cake
football
eat dinner
clean
swim
breakfast
pants
ninth
talk on the phone
in the afternoon
sleep
ride a skateboard
Play ball
seventh
parents
early
lemonade
in the evening
basketball
rope
eat
September
T-shirt
third
jeans
get up
paint
set the
listen to music
table
fly a kite
swimsuit
wash a walk
take a walk
run
draw
jump
ping pong
shorts
speak English
play the guitar
fifty
juice
golf
sixty
cap aunt
niece
July
ninety
May
eighty
cousin
in the morning
first
grandparents
tenth
December
do homework
play the drums
one hundred
sail a boat
tennis
eighth
make a snack
go to school
take pictures
ride a bike
go to
November
go to bed
watch TV
buy snacks